Advent 2

The *LIGHT* shines in
the darkness and
the *darkness*
has *NOT* overcome it.

John 1:5

Advent Goals

Use this season of Advent to challenge your inner spiritual life and by doing so challenge your outer life in your thoughts and actions. Challenge your inner life through spiritual prompts and pathways to prayer. Use this time of Advent through practicing spiritual disciplines to heal your hurts, grow your faith and move closer to God. In doing so challenge your outer life into helping those without homes and those in need.

Advent serves as a time for an anticipation of Christ's birth in the season leading up to Christmas. It can also be a time when we draw closer to God and gave thanks for the gift of his son and display God's love to the world by showing kindness to others.

We often miss Advent's power because the December weeks are full of secular Christmas parties and preparations for Christmas. Each year, the busyness of this season serves to distract us from having an Advent season that truly prepares us for the celebration of Christmas, with all its Christian meaning.

We can miss the importance of Advent, especially as we fall into our culture's concept of Christmas—individualism and consumerism. Instead this Advent, use this time to acknowledge and appreciate God's precious gift to you of his son and practically show gratitude by displaying through your life and works God's love for your community.

The word "Advent" is derived from the Latin word adventus, meaning "coming," During Advent we think about hope, faith, joy, and peace.

At Advent we can celebrate the birth of Jesus as a gift, we can respond to that gift with praise and gratitude, using this season to serve and to give to others.

A popular tradition at Advent is marking the progression of the season through an Advent wreath made up of five candles. This symbol is borrowed from the emphasis in the Bible of Jesus being the Light of the World (Matt. 4:16; John 1:4–9; 8:12). Each week, a new candle is lit in anticipation of Christmas Eve. The last candle, called the Christ Candle, is lit on Christmas Eve to represent Jesus' first advent. Through this theme of ever-increasing light penetrating the darkness, we can see the symbol of God overwhelming the darkness in the world and in our lives.

The season of Advent is one of joy, light and beauty, but sometimes it is overwhelming, dark and hard. Let God's light shine into this season. The power of God's Word is available to help light the way. Prayer can bring peace during this frantic Christmas season.

This Advent let us leave behind the darkness, walk in the light that shines on our path, and renew within ourselves the hope of glory to which he beckons us.

"The celebration of Advent is possible only to those who are troubled in soul, who know themselves to be poor and imperfect, and who look forward to something greater to come." ~ Dietrich Bonhoeffer

Plan with Intention
Sometimes, the endless tasks on our to-do list can end up consuming our time and attention, making it all but impossible to focus on our spiritual life.

With a little intention, we can learn to focus on God as we do these necessary tasks – by praying for the recipients of each gift we wrap, mulling over something we have read as we prepare, or making a mental list of the things we are grateful for while standing in a long line.

What do I want from Advent?
What are we anticipating?
What answer, longing or hope are we waiting for?
How will this Advent change my inner and outer Christian life?

The First Week of Advent

First Sunday of Advent

Sunday 1st December 2024

Today is the first Sunday of Advent. If there was ever a perfect time to reflect on hope, expectations, and our readiness to receive our Saviour once more in our lives, this is the time. Are we ready to welcome Lord as he comes to us?

There's something very special about the first Sunday of Advent — singing the familiar Advent hymns and lighting the first Advent candle. There is a thrill of anticipation that Christmas is just around the corner.

Advent is the season in which believers eagerly anticipate the celebration of Christ's birth. The true meaning of Advent is a time of waiting and preparation and a time to consider more deeply the miracle of the birth of Jesus.

As we enter today the solemn season of Advent in which the Church bids us prepare to celebrate the coming of Christ; let us in this holy season reflect on the coming of Christ who brings light to the world.

Pray

It is indeed right and good to give you thanks and praise, almighty God and everlasting Father,
through Jesus Christ your Son.

For when he humbled himself to come among us in human flesh, he fulfilled the plan you formed before the foundation of the world to open for us the way of salvation.

Confident that your promise will be fulfilled, I now watch for the day when Christ our Lord will come again in glory.

And so I join my voice with angels and archangels and with all the company of heaven to proclaim your glory for ever praising you. Amen

Monday 2ⁿᵈ December 2024

When the Lord comes, he will bring to light the things now hidden in darkness, and will disclose the purposes of the heart. Therefore in the light of Christ let us confess our sins.
cf 1 Corinthians 4.5

Preparing for Advent

What are your spiritual goals for Advent? Write them down

Spiritual Prompt

Have I left enough space in the busy holiday season to pay attention, to listen, to wait, and to be surprised? What practical steps can I take to both guard those quiet moments but also embrace divine interruptions?

Let this Advent be a time of peace for you.

Colossians 3:15 says, "Let the peace of Christ rule in your hearts, since as members of one body you were called to peace. And be thankful."

At Advent we welcome, wait, recognise and embrace God's coming. Events such as the pandemic, a boiling climate and raging wars have created an unsettled world. This Advent we focus on God's coming as the Prince of PEACE.

Pray

A Personal Prayer for Peace
Lord, I invite your peace to rule my heart! As I end this year and reflect on your many gifts you have given me; let my heart be encouraged with the truth that you are a good God. I thank you for sending your Son to die for me. I thank you for the peace I have through you. May my words and actions be ones that glorify you. Amen.

Tuesday 3rd December 2024

During Advent take time to explore different ways to pray. Integrate these patterns of prayer into your daily life.

Praying Imaginatively

Praying imaginatively involves opening our hearts and minds to receive from God in a different way. We do so asking the Holy Spirit to guide and guard us. Imaginative prayer involves entering into a biblical narrative and interacting with the characters in the story, including Jesus or God. Some people do this visually, as if they are in a film. For others it might be more of a journaling experience.

How to Pray with Your Imagination:

Put yourself in a Gospel story or one from the Old Testament. To imagine more easily, choose a story with action instead of one that focuses on Jesus' teaching.

Get comfortable and still yourself, asking God to help you shut down any distractions coming your way. Invite Him to work through your imagination, that His Holy Spirit would fill you and direct you. That He would prevent anything from interfering that is not of Him so that you enjoy freedom in the exercise.

During your time of prayer, you might want to open your hands as a sign of receptivity.

How you enter the story depends on your preferences. For instance, if you can picture things visually, you might want to imagine that you're making a film. Or you might want to consider what sounds you would hear—the roar of the waves, or the murmur of the crowd.

Perhaps you do your best imagining through feeling the emotions, such as the incensed rage of the religious leaders or the desperation of people. Pay attention to the details—the sights, sounds, tastes, smells, and emotions. As you lose yourself in the story, meet Jesus there.

Remember that the aim is to encounter Christ, so try not to get distracted over the historical details—let God take your imagination to reveal something about yourself or Him. And know that exercising your imagination takes practice. It might not come naturally at first, but through persevering you'll find yourself more able to engage. More importantly, remember that God is with you— ask Him through the Holy Spirit to guide you and spark your imagination.

This prayer practice can be done individually or with a group.

Here are some passages suitable for imaginative prayer:

Matthew 14:22-33 (Peter walks on the water)

Mark 10:46-52 (The cure of Bartimaeus)
Luke 5:1-11 (Jesus calls three disciples)
John 13:1-17 (Jesus washes the disciples' feet)
Exodus 3:1-6 (Moses and the burning bush)
1 Samuel 3:1-10 (The call of Samuel)

Action

Charitable Christmas Gift

When your relatives ask you what you want for Christmas, ask them to donate a gift instead. Most charities have a Christmas gift list, which spans chocolates to pyjamas and thermals. Crisis even puts up Amazon wish lists on its website – so it couldn't be easier.

The Big Issue shop is stuffed with goodies from earrings and scarves to bags and candles made by individual crafters, and proceeds go back into the cause. Crisis at Christmas and Centre Point offer the chance to buy a homeless person Christmas dinner. Shelter does a classic range of 30 different Christmas cards in packs of 10, with proceeds from sales going to the charity.

Intentional Kindness

Advent Acts of Kindness.

Each week record an act or acts of kindness. Record your Act of Kindness in your journal.
Try to undertake one deliberate act of kindness.
Move away from the human selfish default setting.
Start slowly, a smile or a nod to someone at the bus stop or in a shop.
It makes their life easier and it makes you feel better.

If something or someone is annoying you don't give an inward grunt but think positively about it and pray about it.

Light-Triggered Prayers

From now until after Christmas, we'll see extra lights just about everywhere—strung over trees, shrubbery, posts and poles, rooflines, and so on.

When your attention is attracted to Advent lights, pray something like, "God, may your light be present in me today." Or, "Jesus, may your love in my life create light for others."

Make up whatever short prayer you want. Allow that light-related phrase to be triggered whenever lights shine on you.

Hymn Phrases

When you hear a Christmas carol, pay attention to the words, and just hold onto a phrase or two for your prayer during the morning's commute or chores around the house.

For instance, maybe you're hearing an instrumental version of "Away in a Manger," a song usually relegated in our minds to the category of children's songs. But here's the final verse to reflect upon.

'Be near me, Lord Jesus, I ask you to stay
close by me forever and love me, I pray.

Bless all the dear children in thy tender care
and fit us for heaven to live with thee there.'

Bible Verses

Spiritual Prompts For Advent

1.   Have I left enough space in the busy holiday season to pay attention, to listen, to wait, and to be surprised? What practical steps can I take to both guard those quiet moments but also embrace divine interruptions?

2.   What am I most grateful for in my life right now?

3.   How did I best serve God this year?

4.   What are my biggest fears, and how can I trust in God to help me overcome them?

5.   What are the blessings in my life that I sometimes take for granted?

6.   How can I prepare myself, my home, and my family for the arrival of Jesus in a way that nurtures a spirit of anticipation and hope?

7.   What are some ways I can share God's love with others during Advent?

8.   How can I deepen my prayer life during the Advent season?

9.   What is one thing I can do to show kindness to others today and each day of Advent?

10.   How am I being called to serve others in my community this Advent?

11.   How do I find more time to pray?

12.   Consider the effects of light. It can warm and it can guide, but it can also expose and surprise. What does light in the darkness mean for you in your life this Advent and for the world?

13.   What lessons have I learned from the challenging experiences I've had this year?

14.   What is one way I can let go of worry and trust in God more?

15.   How can I create more peace in my life and in the world around me this Advent?

16.   What are some things I need to forgive others for, and how can I work towards compassion?

17.   What are my hopes for my spiritual growth in the coming year?

18.   How have I seen God at work in my life recently, and how can I be more aware of His presence?

19.   How can I serve this Advent season?

20.   When I wake up on Christmas morning, how will I be different? How do I hope the meditations and practices of the season will shape me?

Wednesday 4th December 2024

Preparing for Advent
How can I serve this Advent season?
This Advent you are invited to give your time, talents, and treasure to a cause that means something to you. When those who love God work together, great things happen.

Deuteronomy 15:10
You shall give to him freely, and your heart shall not be grudging when you give to him, because for this the Lord your God will bless you in all your work and in all that you undertake.

Action
The Trussell Trust said it has given out 936,000 emergency food parcels to people across the UK between April and September. Giving to a food bank will help many levels of people dealing with poverty, including homeless people. Check which items are needed

at your local food bank before your start.

Pray

God of compassion, your love for humanity was revealed in Jesus, whose earthly life began in the poverty of a stable and ended in the pain and isolation of the cross: I lift up before you those who are homeless and cold especially in the bitter weather of winter. Draw near and comfort them in spirit and bless those who work to provide them with shelter, food and friendship. Show me how I can give of my time, talents and treasure.

Thursday 5th December 2024

Helping The Homeless
Action
The Reverse Advent Calendar
The concept of the reverse advent calendar is to give something away every day instead of getting a little gift from an advent calendar. Add a daily item to a box in the lead-up to Christmas until it is completely filled with food items, clothing and more, then donate it to a food bank or a homeless charity or a person who is homeless who you have befriended and are praying for.

Matthew 25:35-40
For I was hungry and you gave me food, I was thirsty and you gave me drink, I was a stranger and you welcomed me, I was naked and you clothed me, I was sick and you visited me, I was in prison and you came to me.' Then the righteous will answer him, saying, 'Lord, when did we see you hungry and feed you, or thirsty and give you drink? And when did we see you a stranger and welcome you, or naked and clothe you? And when did we see you sick or in prison and visit you?'

Reach Out to Others
While Advent is a time for inner reflection, focusing solely on ourselves tempts us to neglect our call to be good neighbours. St. James spoke very directly about how our faith must ultimately result in action: "Faith of itself, if it does not have works, is dead." Turning

our inward Advent reflections into outward actions shows that God is truly working in our lives.

Pray for Safety for the Homeless
Gracious God I pray for the safety of those without a home including the women and children. Please use Your majestic light to surround them. Let that light keep evil of every kind away from their bodies and minds.

Friday 6th December 2024

Intentional Kindness during Advent
Advent Acts of Kindness.
Each week record an act or acts of kindness. Record your Act of Kindness in your journal.
Undertake one deliberate act of kindness each week.
Move away from the human selfish default setting.
Start slowly, a smile or a nod to someone at the bus stop or in a shop. It makes their life easier and it makes you feel better.
If something or someone is annoying you don't give an inward grunt but think positively about it and pray about it.

Be Still and Know
Be still and know that I am God. Psalm 46 v10

PRAYER is encounter – God's action in us
Find the right place for you – that fits what you need.
The best posture is what leads you to be attentive and relaxed at the same time.

Pray as you can, not as you can't!

"I need to be still and let God love me I need to relax and let God take over" (African American Hymn)

Prayer is a gift.

Sit in a comfortable position – relaxed with back straight.

Concentrate all your attention on the physical feeling of breathing in, then of breathing out. Do not deliberately change your breathing.

Let your in-breath express all that you long for, and your out-breath be a surrender of yourself together with all your worries, anxieties, guilt and pain.

Saturday 7th December 2024

Luke 10:30-37
Jesus replied, "A man was going down from Jerusalem to Jericho, and he fell among robbers, who stripped him and beat him and departed, leaving him half dead. Now by chance a priest was going down that road, and when he saw him he passed by on the other side. So likewise a Levite, when he came to the place and saw him, passed by on the other side. But a Samaritan, as he journeyed, came to where he was, and when he saw him, he had compassion. He went to him and bound up his wounds, pouring on oil and wine. Then he set him on his own animal and brought him to an inn and took care of him. ...

We will have trials and tribulations in this world. Yet, we can find hope in God. No matter what happens, our hope is found in Him. This Advent find hope in God's grace.

John 16:33
"I have told you these things, so that in me you may have peace. ... In this world you will have trouble. ... But take heart! I have overcome the world.".

Hoping

When you thought you had lost your path,

beneath all your fears, I am there

When meaning is gone

I am that meaning

When truth seems hard to find,

I am that truth

When even love seems a bitter thing

I will take that bitter cup from you

And you will taste the wine of my forgiveness

Come back with me to the centre of the things and be held, not torn

Each day is an opportunity for hope

And hope will often arise from those deemed hopeless

Learn to hope in God even when hope seems impossible and beyond

Learn to hope in God's grace even when the rules of the

world cry out that your values have no currency

Learn to hope in God's love

Hope as tender and ephemeral as a new shoot

But which can make the desert bloom and the song birds return.

Richard Carter

The City is my Monastery — A contemporary rule of life.

'Our place of retreat, our monastery, is here and now, where we are today'

Pathways to Prayer
We are always, only a simple word or single step away from a conversation with God.

For those of us struggling with prayer, the Apostle Paul's instruction to "pray constantly" (1 Thessalonians 5:17) may not be as out of reach as we once thought. Here are some ideas for weaving conversational prayer with God into our daily routine. Prayer is a gift from God; praying is a practice. We are only ever a word away from a conversation with God. Sometimes it can be hard.
As disciples of Jesus, we long to pray our own words and share what is on our minds and hearts. In prayer, we bring our pain, hopes, joys, and fears to God in a personal way.

These ways to pray draw from the deep well of Christian history to make praying a habit to enjoy in our busy and wearying times.

1. Praying with the Bible
There are different ways to use your Bible in your prayer time. You can personalise Scripture by putting your own name into a verse. For example, "Amy, my peace I leave with you … Amy, do not let your heart be troubled." (John 14:27) Try writing out a prayer from the Bible, adapting it into your own words. Or write the words of Scripture into a poem, just using the key words.

2. Pair Up.
Form a prayer partnership with a fellow Christ-follower. Take turns giving each other a call every day, and spend a few minutes praying together about the day to come. The call may only take a few minutes, but it will do wonders for your ability to hear God's voice throughout the day.

3. Praying through the Bible
Lectio divina is Latin for sacred reading. The practice of going repeatedly through a short section of Scripture has been used for more than a thousand years. There are 4 steps—reading, meditating, praying, and contemplating. Each time you go through the Bible passage, take time to pause, notice, and interact with the Holy Spirit.

4. Listen
Rather than listening to your regular playlists as you walk, listen to worship songs or hymns. Focus on the lyrics, and let the songs inspire you to pray as you go, confessing any sins and inviting God to spend the day with you.

5. Practicing the Presence of God
Practicing the presence of God can be done anywhere and at any time. It's simply calling to mind that God dwells within us through His Spirit and His Son. Being aware of God in our daily lives requires being intentional and aware. Welcome Jesus into whatever you are doing. You might want to set a timer at various intervals to remind yourself to call to mind the presence of Jesus.

Second Sunday of Advent

2ND SUNDAY OF Advent

Sunday 8th December 2024

1 Kings 19

11 The Lord said, "Go out and stand on the mountain in the presence of the Lord, for the Lord is about to pass by."

Then a great and powerful wind tore the mountains apart and shattered the rocks before the Lord, but the Lord was not in the wind. After the wind there was an earthquake, but the Lord was not in the earthquake. 12 After the earthquake came a fire, but the Lord was not in the fire. And after the fire came a gentle whisper. 13 When Elijah heard it, he pulled his cloak over his face and went out and stood at the mouth of the cave.

Then a voice said to him, "What are you doing here, Elijah?"

After reading the passage, consider where God is, and where God isn't, for you? What are the things you need to retreat from, in order to move forward?

'The Spirit of God is present in our quiet moments'
Spend a few minutes as still and quiet as you can find, listening to your own breathing, conscious that this is the sound of the spirit of God working in you.

This Advent let us leave behind the darkness of sin, walk in the light that shines on our path, and renew within ourselves the hope of glory to which he beckons us.

You may like to end with this prayer, before you continue with your day.

Pray
Grant me the grace, O Lord, to turn my attention inward and behold the miracle of my breath. May I recognise it as the gentle rhythm of life, woven with sacred threads and the dirt of the earth, a sacred tether connecting me to the divine source of life.

God of hope, I look to you with an open heart and yearning spirit. During this Advent season, I will keep alert and awake, listening for your word and keeping to your principles. My hope is in you.

Open my heart and mind to perceive the truths whispered by my breath. Illuminate the paths I tread this Advent and grant me the wisdom to follow in Your path towards Your kingdom. Amen

Monday 9ᵗʰ December 2024
Are you at a crossroads in your life?
Advent provides a space for people at a crossroads in life to pause, step back and reflect on where they are, the questions they need to answer, what they really want and how to take steps forward.

Jeremiah 6:16
"Stand at the crossroads and look. Look for the ancient paths. Ask where the good way is and walk in it and you will find rest for your soul."

The crossroads could be vocational, such as a career change, or relational, such as divorce or separation. It could be a significant interruption in life from a change of circumstances or health, or simply a sense of wanting something different from life.

We just have to learn to 'stand', to 'look', to 'ask', to 'walk'

Stand: To pause and breathe and come out of our busyness and preoccupations

Look: To look with bare attention at what is happening and how it is feeling right now in our lives

Ask: To enquire more deeply about what we really want, what we know in our heart is needed right now.

Walk: To find the clarity, calm and courage to do what really matters.

'The function of prayer is not to influence God but rather to change the nature of one who prays'. Soren Kierkegaard

Pray

Ask God to give you guidance and show you what and who to pray for.

Blessed are you, Lord God of all creation,
Who still brings light from darkness, and order from chaos,
and who gives that peace which the world cannot give;

As I seek the signs of your presence in my midst, keep me attentive to the beauty and brokenness of your world and strengthen my heart and mind, and hands and voice that I may work for your justice, show your mercy and walk with humility and confidence in the paths of righteousness and peace, that the whole creation may rejoice and sing your praise.

Blessed be God, Father, Son and Holy Spirit.
Blessed be God for ever.

People to Pray For

Hopes & Fears

Tuesday 10th December 2024
Spiritual Prompt For Advent

Have I lost my way?

Sometimes something happens to us that turns our life upside down. It feels that along our life's journey, we have 'lost our way'.

There are times when we become aware that the way we are living our lives no longer feels quite right. We may experience a mixture of emotions – perhaps we feel directionless, life feels a bit pointless and we lack that zest for life we used to have when we were younger.

Or perhaps we find ourselves overwhelmed. Maybe we sense there is more to us than we know, we have potential that is not being fully realised.

These feelings can be upsetting but they can also be the most fertile times in our lives. It is time to stop, look and listen to God.

We need to take time to reflect.

Pray and ask: what does God want for me?

Wednesday 11th December 2024

Finding Stillness

Psalm 46:10
Be still, and know that I am God

Use this time of Advent to help you find a place of calm within you that allows you to be less reactive and more aware of your choices in life.

Use this time of Advent to give you the opportunity to find real space in your life, to reconnect to what really matters to you and equip you with simple everyday practices that help you strengthen and maintain an inner peace and stillness in the face of whatever life throws at you.

Take time.
Close your eyes.
Open your hands.
Breathe in 'God Loves Me'
Breathe out 'Praise Your Name'

'Prayer, in my opinion, is nothing else than an intimate sharing between friends; it means taking time frequently to be alone with Him who we know loves us.' - Teresa of Avila

Thursday 12th December 2024

Daily Meditation Practice

An important step in our day is to build in a time of prayer. Think of this as a check in call to God to ensure that everything is fine. A daily prayer time can build stability into our daily life.

When we create a pattern for ourselves and exercise the discipline of prayer in our daily routine and maintain it over time, we create for ourselves something that will centre us in God.

The key thing is consistency.

Everyone's day will be different, but there are three times when it's helpful to spend time in thoughtful prayer - on waking up, the middle of our day, and before we go to sleep.

Taking a few minutes for a short meditative prayer to reflect on how what is happening to us or how we are feeling can provide a strong foundation for finding stillness in our life.

Moreover, once a routine has been established, if there is a crisis then with our prayer muscle memory in place, we can automatically turn to God for reassurance and support. This can give us courage and stop us from being overwhelmed.

Prayers

Advent Reflections

Friday 13th December 2024
Peace

Colossians 3:15-17
Let the peace of Christ rule in your hearts, since as members of one body you were called to peace. And be thankful. Let the message of Christ dwell among you richly as you teach and admonish one another with all wisdom through psalms, hymns, and songs from the Spirit, singing to God with gratitude in your hearts. And whatever you do, whether in word or deed, do it all in the name of the Lord Jesus, giving thanks to God the Father through Him.

Prepare
During Advent we don't always take the time to prepare for Jesus' birth as we would prepare for Easter during Lent. Think of ways we can be still and prepare for Christmas and Jesus's birth. Write down one way in which you will seek to be still in the coming weeks: whether it's through journaling or setting an alarm as a reminder to pray or maybe going for a meditative walk .

Pray

Dear God, help me to prepare for Advent. Please grant me your peace.

Saturday 14th December 2024

Pathway to prayer
Keeping a Journal
Writing down our prayers every day in a notebook can help us focus and help our concentration. When you look back over your writing, you can reflect on how God was with you and how your prayers were answered.

Amid our frenetic pace of life, keeping a prayer journal is an invaluable means of grace in our Christian walk and a practical discipline with many benefits. Vital to making your prayer journal serve your spiritual vibrancy, is saturating it with Bible verses that speak to you in your particular circumstances and permeating it with prayer. You do not have to spend hours on this. Even a tiny change in your life, of giving a few minutes every day in prayer and contemplation can change your life. Keeping a daily journal can be an aid to prayer and meditation.

Journaling helps to persevere in the journey you are on with Christ and it also helps to open up to God. It helps you to be more honest with God and with yourself. Keeping a journal can be powerful. It is cathartic. It can empty your mind and give you peace. It feels good to get all of those thoughts and feelings out of your head and down on paper. The world seems clearer. You are calmer and feel better.

Pray
Write down what is on your mind today and tell God about it.

Pathways to Prayer
1. Show & Tell.
Decorate your room or work space with art or photography that inspires you to turn your attention to God. Hang the art where you will see it often, and let it serve as a reminder to renew your connection with God's presence.

2. Hearing God
Our Bibles burst with God speaking to His children, from Genesis to Revelation. One well-loved example of God's communication with young Samuel in 1 Samuel 3. Samuel needed help from Eli, at first, to understand God. As we practice listening prayer, we can test what we hear from God with three helps: Scripture, impressions of the Holy Spirit, and circumstances. Think about having a quiet time or even a retreat away from the bustle of your life to concentrate on listening and discerning what God wants to say to you. To hear God, try being quiet and still.

3. Keep a Prayer Journal
Writing down your prayers every day in a notebook can help you focus and help your concentration. When you look back over your writing, you can reflect on how God was with you and how your prayers were answered.

4. Praying with Lament

Our prayer book in the Bible, the Psalms, bursts with songs of lament, not only those written by individuals but those for corporate worship. The psalmists cry out to God, asking and even demanding that He help them. The psalmists often move through their lament in four stages: address, complaint, request and expression of trust. Follow this pattern to pen your own prayer of lament.

5. Nature Walk.

Engaging with nature is a great way to deepen our connection with God. Take a break from your routine and go somewhere with trees and grass. Take off your shoes and let your heart connect with the beauty of the natural world. Invite God to join you as you walk.

6. Praying Imaginatively

Praying imaginatively involves opening our hearts and minds to receive from God in a different way. We do so asking the Holy Spirit to guide and guard us. Imaginative prayer involves entering into a biblical narrative and interacting with the characters in the story, including Jesus or God. Some people do this visually, as if they are in a film. For others it might be more of a journaling experience.

7. Think On This.

One of the most ancient of the spiritual disciplines, meditation, is also one of the most portable. On index cards, write three or four verses or short passages from the Bible and tape them to your desk. As you notice the cards, be reminded to take a minute or two to talk with God about what they say. Rotate new verses in regularly to keep the conversation fresh.

8. Praying the Examen

Ignatius, founder of the Jesuit order of priests, practiced a five-step process called the examen: give thanks, ask, review, repent, renew. The regular practice of the examen can free us from the effects of unconfessed sin. With the examen we can also become more sensitive to discerning God's voice and moving forward with Him, as we reject our sinful desires.

9. Focus In.

As you run your errands or perform those mindless chores we all face each week, turn it into a time of silent focus. Make the commitment to stay quiet, to move slowly, and to focus your attention on listening. Don't speak. Instead, let God direct the conversation in your heart.

10. Knowing God is There No Matter What
Put a hand or both hands to the side of your face. You cannot see your hands but you know that they are there. Sometimes we feel so far from God and so marooned with trouble that we think we have lost God in our life but just as you know the hands are there, although you cannot see them, know that God is with you during this grim time.

11. Quiet Time.
Each day set aside a time for you and God to be with each other in private prayer. Look out for retreats or quiet days offered by your church.

12. Intentional Praying
When you are out and about walking, and you see a piece of litter, pick it up and praise God for his goodness.

13. Gratitude
Each day spend a little time saying thank you and counting your blessings.

14. Intercessory Prayers
Intercessory prayer is the act of praying to God on behalf of others. This can be for individuals or for situations. There are so many challenging situations across the world.

Ask God to place a country or situation on your heart. Spend some time listening and reflecting on what he shares with you. Begin by acknowledging God's power.

Then pray general prayers: pray for God's kingdom to come and pray for individuals and communities.

The city is my monastery
We plan the holiday in advance
But the holy day is today
The monks knew the ancient wisdom of giving each part of
the day to God
So that they tasted the height, breadth and depth of God's
presence
The coming of the light, the hopes and struggles of the day,
the intensity of noon,
the shadows of evening bringing the toil to an end,
food and refreshment, the silence and darkness of the night
But we no longer notice the movements of the sun
We do not see the sky just the screen
We have used the remote and become remote
We who have no time for God
Have become time's prisoners
We have pulled the curtains on the sun and moon and have
closed the windows so that we no
longer smell the rain or breathe the air of the changing
seasons
We have been given this treasure beyond price and yet we
scarcely notice it.
Our monastery is here and now
Where you are today
The person you are speaking with
The room you are sitting in
The street where you are walking
The action you are doing now
This is your monastery
This is your prayer
Eternity is now
The city is our monastery.
In each person there is a portion of solitude which no
human intimacy can ever fill

Yet you are never alone
Let yourself be plummeted to the depths
And you will see that in your heart of hearts

In the place where no two people are alike
Christ is waiting for you
And what you never dared hope for springs to life.'

Richard Carter

The City is my Monastery — A contemporary rule of life.

'Our place of retreat, our monastery, is here and now, where
we are today'

During Advent, we can turn off the noise — the
news, the socials, the music — and just sit in
silence before God.

Tell God what you are waiting for this Advent.

Hope

What hopes have you this Advent?

Third Sunday of Advent

3RD SUNDAY (OF) *Advent*

Sunday 15ᵗʰ December 2024

During this solemn season of Advent in which the Church bids us prepare to celebrate the coming of Christ; a coming that we recall in the Child of Bethlehem; a coming that we experience in the gift of his Spirit, in the bread of the Eucharist, in the joy of human lives that are shared; a coming we wait for when God gathers up all things in Christ. Let turn towards the light and as we turn towards the light, let us have on our hearts all those who see no light, for whom all is darkness and despair. Let us pray that they too may be illumined by Christ who is our light.

Pray

It is indeed right and good to give you thanks and praise, almighty God and everlasting Father,
through Jesus Christ your Son.

He is the one foretold by all the prophets, whom the Virgin Mother bore with love beyond all telling.

John the Baptist was his herald and made him known when at last he came.

In his love, Christ fill me with joy as I prepare to celebrate your birth, so that when you come again you may find me watching in prayer, with my heart filled with wonder and praise.

And so, with angels and archangels, and with all the company of heaven, I proclaim your glory.

I pray for those who see no light, for whom all is darkness and despair. Amen

Monday 16th December 2024

Spiritual Prompt For Advent
How did I best serve God this year?

1 Timothy 6:17-19
As for the rich in this present age, charge them not to be haughty, nor to set their hopes on the uncertainty of riches, but on God, who richly provides us with everything to enjoy. They are to do good, to be rich in good works, to be generous and ready to share, thus storing up treasure for themselves as a good foundation for the future, so that they may take hold of that which is truly life.

1 Corinthians 16:14
Let all that you do be done in love.

Luke 3:11
And he answered them, "Whoever has two tunics is to share with him who has none, and whoever has food is to do likewise."

There are many charities doing great work in helping homeless people to rebuild their lives. Money goes on counselling, life skills courses, legal support and more, and charities are always in need of donations – in most cases these can be made online. Try St James's Church Piccadilly, St Mungo's, Centrepoint Homeless Charity, Shelter, The Salvation Army, Crisis, Help the Homeless, or sign up for a subscription of The Big Issue – its new mapping tool allows you to locate a homeless person in your area and help them directly with 50 per cent of the price of a mag going directly them.

Action : Donate Money

There are two conflicting schools of thought on this. Some believe giving money directly to a homeless person is the best course of action, as some of the money you give to charity can end up going into administration costs. Others believe that giving money directly to the recipients perpetuates destructive cycles, and giving money to charity is more effective in the long run, getting people permanently off the streets.

Pray for those with no homes

Father, please help the people who have no homes. Lord God Almighty, protect them from harm.
Gracious God, please guide me to notice when someone needs help, and guide me to give help. Please help me to know how to provide comfort and aid.

Tuesday 17th December 2024

2 Thessalonians 3:16 says, "Now may the Lord of peace himself give you peace at all times and in every way. The Lord be with all of you."

Instead of frantically running in all directions, God tells us to be still, and know that he is God. He is still the ultimate ruler, our problems and troubles are just opportunities for him to be exalted among the nations, it is also an opportunity for us to re-learn that the Lord of hosts is with us.

Pray

Just breathe
Breathe in and breathe out. Breathe in and then say something to God that is concerning you.
Then breathe out and say 'be still, and know that I am God'.

'Breathe in: there are people who are desperate to find a safe place to sleep. Breathe out: be still, and know that I am God'.

'Breathe in: migrants are desperate to find a safe place to survive. Breathe out: be still, and know that I am God'.

'Breathe in: people who are struggling financially need help. Breathe out: be still, and know that I am God …'

Wednesday 18th December 2024

Galatians 2:10
Only, they asked us to remember the poor, the very thing I was eager to do.

Galatians 6:10
So then, as we have opportunity, let us do good to everyone, and especially to those who are of the household of faith.

Spiritual Prompt for Advent
Have you considering going on a retreat? Throughout the ages, the Christian tradition has understood Retreat to be an important part of spiritual formation. As followers of Jesus we know that retreat is not an escape from reality but an engagement with all that is most real and most important in life. It is a time to gain perspective on our relationship to God, on the church and the world around us. It can be a time of challenge but also a time of reward.

Finding Stillness

Psalm 46:10
Be still, and know that I am God

Use this time of Advent to help you find a place of calm within you that allows you to be less reactive and more aware of your choices in life.

Here in stillness
Here as you breathe in deeply
Let the presence of God release you
And fill you with his peace

Like rain on dry land
Like sunlight's warming brightness in the cold
Feel again the flow of God's life flowing in and out
Untangling you from the inside out

Thursday 19th December 2024

James 2:16
And one of you says to them, "Go in peace, be warmed and filled," without giving them the things needed for the body, what good is that?

Proverbs 28:27
Whoever gives to the poor will not want, but he who hides his eyes will get many a curse.

Intentional Kindness during Advent

Advent Acts of Kindness.
Each week record an act or acts of kindness. Record your Act of Kindness in your journal.
Undertake one deliberate act of kindness today.
Move away from the human selfish default setting.
Start slowly, a smile or a nod to someone at the bus stop or in a shop. It makes their life easier and it makes you feel better.
If something or someone is annoying you, don't give an inward grunt, but think positively about it and pray about it.

Pray

Lord, please provide food, shelter and medical care for those who are in need. Please encourage me to make a difference. Heavenly Father, open my eyes and ears to notice anyone who is in need and show me ways to help.

Friday 20th December 2024

John 14:27

"Peace I leave with you; my peace I give to you. Not as the world gives do I give to you. Let not your hearts be troubled, neither let them be afraid."

As we approach the celebration of the birth of Jesus, let's reflect on the things that rule our hearts right now. If it's not peace, let's be honest with ourselves and realise that the gift of peace is real and we can take hold of it and elevate Jesus to his rightful place as ruler of our hearts, letting peace envelop our lives.

Pray

Loving God, I declare that you are first in my life. Thank you for coming to earth so I can experience the gift of peace.

Help me to recognise your peace in the busyness of my day, enjoying this sacred moment of communion with you.

Stop me in my tracks if need be, so that I can open myself up to you. In Jesus' name. Amen

Saturday 21st December 2024
Helping The Homeless

Luke 14:13-14
But when you give a feast, invite the poor, the crippled, the lame, the blind, and you will be blessed, because they cannot repay you. For you will be repaid at the resurrection of the just."

Pray for the Homeless at Christmas

Gracious Jesus, during this joyful season, let me remember those who do not have a stable roof over their heads.

Please give them peace this year as they do their best to get through the holiday season. Remind them of Your promises, keep hope in their hearts, and guide me to meet their needs as best as I can.

Faith

Are you lacking in faith?

How can you strengthen your faith?

How do I hope the meditations and practices of the season of Advent will shape me?

Have I left enough space in the busy Advent season to pay attention, to listen, to wait, and to be surprised? What practical steps can I take to both guard those quiet moments but also embrace divine interruptions?

Sunday 22nd December 2024

Some churches have a 'Blue Christmas' service just before Christmas.

The 'Blue Christmas' service is a recognition and a public assurance that Christmas is emphatically not about enforced jollity or pressure to be 'on form'. But an equal assurance that in celebrating the incarnation, there is, in the words of the old carol, 'comfort and joy' that is possible when the ancient wisdom of Scripture bursts into life with the shocking gospel that God is with us.

There is a 'being swept up in it all' about Christmas. Not allowing ourselves to be distracted by or obsessed with the consumerism, competitive catering, anxiety-provoking socialising that is the seed material of a thousand stand-up comics. But placing ourselves in the way of that story: hearing again the awesome reality of incarnation, of the presence and love of the divine being unalterably and irresistibly poured out into the world that was hurting so much then and is hurting now. And that the way that love is poured out is into a vulnerable thin-skinned child whose very presence made grown adults, even wise ones, fall to their knees in wonder. And pray, and cry in relief, and give of what they had.

Even, and perhaps especially when despair is near, we are invited at Christmas to fall on our knees and pray in thanksgiving for all the gifts we have, and acknowledge our impulse to give to others in response. Pray for forgiveness for our sins of negligence, ignorance and wilful self-interest. And, as part of our response, offer what we have, which is our open-heartedness every day, together. And from within that context of gifts in which we live, remember our capacity for awe and wonder, and offer to God too our repentance, which is our determination to change.

Pray

For the gifts I have.
For forgiveness for my sins of negligence, ignorance and wilful self-interest.
I offer all that I have.
I repent.
I am determined to change.

Joy

What brings you joy? Make a list.
How can you bring joy to others?

Peace

Where are you lacking peace?

For each item you wrote, separate out the circumstance using the FACETS model:

F   What are the facts? If an outside observer were describing the situation, what would they say?

A   What actions are you taking? (include reactions, not just intentional actions here)

C   What is the context? (ongoing circumstances relevant to this issue)

E   What emotions do you notice regarding this issue?

T   What thoughts do you have about this issue? (include the irrational ones – it is especially important to notice those)

S   What body sensations do you notice when you think about this issue?

What is getting in the way of feeling at peace. You may want to write some action steps based on whatever comes up in this exercise.

Monday 23rd December 2024

In these serious and perilous times, this Christmas, the incarnation – God with us in the defenceless child Jesus – gives us a picture of vulnerability, yes, but also a promise of resilient and enduring love. God who comes both undefended and undefeated.

The beginning of the good news about Jesus the Messiah, the Son of God, as it is written in Isaiah the prophet: 'I will send my messenger ahead of you, who will prepare your way'" - Mark 1:1-2 NIV

Then I heard the VOICE of the Lord saying, "Whom shall I send? And who will go for us?" And I said, "Here am I. Send me!" - Isaiah 6:8

This grace was given to us in Christ Jesus before the ages began, but it has now been revealed through the appearing of our Savior Jesus Christ." - 2 Timothy 1:9-10 NRSVUE

"Restore us, God Almighty; make your face shine on us, that we may be saved." - Psalm 80:7 NIV

TAIZÉ CHANT
Within our darkest night, you kindle the fire that never dies away, that never dies away.
Within our darkest night, you kindle the fire that never dies way, that never dies away.

Spirit of God, calm the turmoil in our souls so that we can hear your still small voice.

Pray

I pray for all those who experience the absence of God in their lives this Christmas and for those fearful of believing that God may yet come.

I pray for all those who grieve this Christmas, for those who lament all that used to be and cannot be anymore after the loss of a loved one, a home, a job or a cause.

I pray for all those who are homeless, lonely at home or far from home this Christmas, for the cold and hungry, and all who feel they are on the outside looking in.

I pray for those who cannot give voice or words to the trauma they have suffered and the pain they still feel.

Spirit of God, surround us all with your presence and your peace, and comfort all who feel abandoned, forsaken or forgotten.

Spirit of God, accept the silence of my worship and heal any hurting hearts.

TAIZÉ CHANT
Our darkness is never darkness in your sight.
The deepest night is clear as the daylight.

Tuesday 24ᵗʰ December 2024 Christmas Eve

John 1:4-5:
"In him was life, and that life was the light of all mankind. The light shines in the darkness, and the darkness has not overcome it."

Today we anticipate the birth of Jesus. For many it will be a busy day, but in the midst of the bustle take a moment to give thanks. Let us remember the promises of Advent in our lives, the promises of peace, faith and hope.

This Christmas Eve and Day we can light a fifth central candle that reminds us of the light that shines in the darkness! This light shines in the darkness but the darkness shall not overpower it (John 1:5).

Pray
As I await my coming Saviour, let me be at peace and love and serve the Lord. Let the light of the world shine through my life.
In the name of The Lord Jesus Christ. Amen.

Blessing
May the God of grace and glory light the spark of love in your heart. And the blessing of God who created, redeemed and inspired you from the beginning, be with you this Christmas season and for ever.

Wednesday 25th December 2024 *Christmas Day*

Happy Christmas

The child has been born; the angels are singing their song of peace, the mysterious visitors from the east are still on their way. But far from being 'over', the festival of Christmas has only just begun. There are 12 days ahead now on which to let it all sink in, take this time to see what it all might mean.

Pray
I give thanks for the gift of Christ to the world. I rejoice in the love that the good news of this birth brings to a waiting world.

I pray :
For all people carrying fear and anxiety.
For all who are in another intensive period of work in the NHS, in care homes, in social care, in shops and public transport.
For all whose lives are in perpetual lockdown, confined by poverty or fear, illness or isolation.
For all decision makers, business leaders, local and national politicians
God of mercy and light. Hear my prayers.
God of glory, God of peace, God of hope, guide my steps as I make my way through days that are not only festive but fearful. Help me take account of the anxiety I feel without letting it overwhelm my joy that Christ is born in my heart. Amen.

Blessing
At the beginning, at the end, at this moment in between, in these best and worst of times:
Now is the time in which God creates,
Now is the time in which God heals,
Now is the time in which Christ comes.
May the life of the Christ child given for this broken, yet beautiful world be born anew this day.
And the blessing of God: Creator, Redeemer and Spirit of Life be with and remain with you.

Thoughts & Prayers

Thanks & Praise

Prayers For Others

Thursday 26th December 2024   St Stephen's Day

Today, as the Christmas carol describes it, is the 'Feast of Stephen' or St Stephen's Day, also known as Boxing Day.

That we mark the feast of Stephen today right after the birth of Jesus is one of the ways Christian faith is saved from floating off into a spiritual realm that is not anchored in life as it's lived. If we've been fortunate enough to have had a Christmas Day with good food and company, then Boxing Day or St Stephen's Day can feel a bit of an anticlimax. The boxes of boxing day come from a time when servants were given the day off after cooking for the celebrations of their masters, and given a box of treats to take home to their own families.

Today we think about those unsung heroes who just get on with it: our local communities and societies are enriched hugely by people who do that, running sports clubs or lunch clubs, after school activities or dementia cafes. People who help knit us together, give us somewhere to be, help us eat together or make friends, build community and give a helping hand to someone else who needs it today. A message of today: we discover that it's quite a simple meaning: it's about living a life that puts others needs before our own.

Pray

Today, Loving God I remember the unsung heroes in my community. I name some of them to you now. Thank you for their work and their presence. They are the salt of the earth. Please God, help me to live a life that puts the needs of others before my own.

Wednesday 27th December 2024

Take time to remember those who have not had a great Christmas. Those without work, unable to afford to join in much of the usual social activity of society. Or for some older people who are unable to leave their homes. Into some of the bleakest reflections about our society, come the Christmas lights, the sleigh bells, the tinsel and the music. But for some, maybe even you, there is a mismatch not just this Christmas but most Christmases, it can feel as if the festivity of Christmas lights are being strung up across life circumstances as bleak as a grey stone-hard pavement.

All is not lost, this is where the deepest hope is found in the message of Christmas. Because as fun as they are, the birth of Christ doesn't need, nor didn't feature, the glossy colours of a 21st century decoration, so the meaning is not affected if those decorations are not there or unseen. Perhaps one of the profoundest conclusions that Christians draw from the festival of Christmas, *is that God is with us. Remember that wherever we are and however things are God is not far away, but near. God is not remote, shouting instructions to us across some sort of cosmic divide, but God is there with us, involved in the mess of our life.*

Pray

Thank you God for the gift of your son Jesus Christ. Thank you God for being with me in the messiness of my life. Thank you God that I can rely on you whatever the situation. Thank you that all is not lost, that I have the deepest hope, found in the message of Christmas. I give you praise.

Thursday 28th December 2024

Matthew 5:16
In the same way, let your light shine before others, that they may see your good deeds and glorify your Father in heaven.

Light is used to symbolise God, faith, and holiness throughout the Bible. As Christians, we are called to not only walk in the light but to be the light for others.

Some find the kind of wintry grey light of December and January depressing. There is a flatness about the light at this time of year that others find restful and comforting. It's all part of the variety of God's creation, a rest somehow from the glamour and attention given to gorgeous sunsets or high noon.

Prayer can be a powerful tool for self-reflection and change. It can help us to see our lives through the lens of our faith, and to understand our goals and challenges in a new light.

Prayer can also give us the strength and courage we need to make positive changes in our lives.

At the end of the year, taking some time to pray can be a helpful way to reflect on the past year and to set our intentions for the year ahead.

Pray
Mighty God, thank you for sending your Son to be the light that pierces the darkness that covers this world. This year has felt darker, harder, and heavier for the world. Please grant me the faith and hope to hold unto you no matter what lies ahead. Help me to reflect on the year that has past and set my intentions for the year ahead.

Friday 29th December 2024
John 8:12
When Jesus spoke again to the people, he said, "I am the light of the world. Whoever follows me will never walk in darkness, but will have the light of life."

The presence of God in the world and in a human life is often described with reference to light. But it matters what kind of light. We human beings can make mistakes about this. We're often too easily impressed by light that draws attention only to itself. The light that signals God's presence, by contrast, doesn't draw your eye only to itself, but it illuminates, reveals, bathes. It is not a brash searchlight sort of harshness that thoughtlessly exposes our attention to the intrusive gaze of others. The light of Christ's presence in the world, celebrated at Christmas, is recognised by its generosity, beauty and capacity to help us understand and appreciate more deeply what it is to be alive, to be surrounded by gifts freely given and unearned. And in the light of that knowledge, give of ourselves in return.

Pray
Gracious God, thank You for being the light in my life. Let me act in such a way that others can see that light.

Loving God, thank You for Your faithfulness and love. I praise You for all the blessings You have given me this year, both big and small. I ask that You would continue to watch over me and guide me in the coming year.

Saturday 30th December 2024
Pathways To Prayer

Lectio Divina
A form of prayer is Lectio Divina (Latin for "Divine Reading") which is a contemplative way to read the Bible. It is a way of praying through the scriptures. You imagine yourself in the bible passage. It is a traditional monastic practice of scriptural reading, meditation and prayer intended to promote communion with God and to increase the knowledge of the Bible. It is not a Bible study of a passage. Lectio Divina consists of four steps:

Lectio (reading),
Oratio (praying),
Meditatio (meditation), and
Contemplatio (contemplating).

It is a way of praying the Bible that leads us deeper into God's word. We slow down. We read a short passage more than once. We mull it over slowly and carefully. We savour it. The Scripture begins to speak to us in a new way. It speaks to us personally, and aids that union we have with God through Christ who is himself the Living Word.

Fr Christopher Jamison, former Abbot of Worth Abbey in Sussex, England in his book Finding Sanctuary writes of three key features of Lectio Divina:

The first is that "the text is seen as a gift to be received, not a problem to be dissected.... let the text come to you."

The second is that the lectio tradition "teaches us that in order to receive what the text has to offer we must read slowly."

The third is that lectio is "a way of prayer. Before reading, pray that

God will speak to you through the text. During reading, allow the reading to evolve into meditation and then into prayer and finally contemplation.

When the reading is concluded, keep some phrase in mind and repeat it throughout the day so that prayerful reading becomes prayerful living."

Try using Lectio Divina with the miracles of Jesus.

Sunday 31st December 2024 New Year's Eve
Looking Back
We are on the other side now of Christ's birth – the waiting for his arrival is over, but the reality is we are still waiting for His second coming. Advent can be looked at as a season to look back and one to look forward—preparing for Jesus' second coming.

As you look back over December what did the season of Advent bring to your Christian life?

As you look back over this last year ask yourself how has God used me this year in the lives of others?

What do my resources (time, talent, finances, attitude, thoughts, passions) say about my focus and priorities this past year?

Are you fulfilling the deepest human vocation by learning to serve God by putting other people's needs before your own? We're asked to love our neighbour as ourselves. That's it; it's as simple and difficult as that.

Pray
Lord, Whether I leave behind a year of joy or of trials and difficulties, I pause to give thanks. Thank you for being with me every day of every year. Thank you for making all things new and for giving me the grace of fresh starts and new beginnings. Help me to learn from last year and put you at the centre of my life in the year to come.

Prayer Bowl

Choose a bowl, basket, or box that you can set in a central spot in your home. If this will be a family activity, you might place the container on the table where you have your meals or on a shelf near where you enter or exit your home. If you are doing this by yourself, then place the container on your dresser or some spot in the house you walk by frequently.

On small cards or slips of paper, write names—one name per card—of friends, family, and others you want to pray for. Every day pick a name and keep that name with you throughout the day, in a pocket or somewhere you'll notice it and be reminded to pray specifically for that person.

You could make this a family project, keeping the names in a dish on the dinner table and every day praying as a family for the person whose name you picked.

Lessons from Looking Back

Christian Goals for 2025

1st January 2025
Looking Forward

2 Corinthians 5:17
"Therefore, if anyone is in Christ, he is a new creation. The old has passed away; behold, the new has come".

Jeremiah 29:11 tells us, "for I know the plans I have for you," declares the Lord, "plans to prosper you and not to harm you, plans to give you hope and a future."

Spiritual Prompts for the New Year

In which spiritual discipline do I most want to make progress this year?

The practice of spiritual disciplines for personal spiritual growth includes Bible study, prayer, meditation, and fasting. These are referred to as inward disciplines. Outward practices are service, solitude, submission, and simplicity, while corporate practices are worship, celebration and guidance.

What's the most important way, by God's grace, I will try to make this year different from last?

What do I want to see God do in my life this coming year? What areas of my life do I want Him to transform, reshape, or change?

Pray
Loving God, thank You for making all things new.

As another new year begins, help me live each day for You. May I continually have a new song in my heart to sing to You, no matter what comes my way.

I trust in You because I know that Your mercies are new every morning, and I pray for faith to know that you are always by my side. Please reveal your will for me in this new year.

Making a Difference in 2025

Thoughts & Prayers

2nd January 2025

Psalms 7

1 LORD my God, I take refuge in you; save and deliver me from all who pursue me,

10 My shield is God Most High, who saves the upright in heart.

17 I will give thanks to the LORD because of his righteousness; I will sing the praises of the name of the LORD Most High.

Is there someone in your life that seems to make a point of not getting along with you?

Have you ever encountered someone intent on bringing you down—spiritually or emotionally?

Try to find someone you trust that you can talk to. There are a number of confidential telephone services that will be able to listen to you.

Pray

Mighty God, I bring before you this problem I am having. You know my struggles. Please help me.

Prayer Practice

Place a hand to each side of your face.
You cannot see your hands but you know they are there.
You cannot see God but have the faith to know that he is there.
Tell him what is troubling you.

Please leave a review for this book.

The Merton Prayer

My Lord God,
I have no idea where I am going.
I do not see the road ahead of me.
I cannot know for certain where it will end.

Nor do I really know myself, and the fact
that I think I am following your will
does not mean that I am actually doing so.

But I believe that the desire to please you
does in fact please you.

And I hope I have that desire in all
that I am doing.

I hope that I will never do anything
apart from that desire.

And I know that if I do this, you will
lead me by the right road, though I
may know nothing about it.

Therefore will I trust you always
though I may seem to be lost and in
the shadow of death.

I will not fear, for you are ever with me,
and you will never leave me to
face my perils alone.

Thomas Merton

Advent draws attention both to the estrangement between heaven and earth, and the promise that this state of estrangement is not forever. The incarnation itself, the coming of Christ into the world, is a lovingly-sewed stitch that starts to bring together the edges of this great wound, and in these times we need to recognise that to participate in God's justice for the world means participating in God's love for the world. Almost every aspect of the ecological crisis that we face has been caused by what one might term 'materialism': the relentless and careless consumption of the precious gifts that earth brings forth, and the commodification and exploitation of people and planet.

We have not loved the world and all that is in it as fiercely and as totally as God loves it and for too long we have failed to acknowledge the real dignity and value of all that God has made. We are part of creation, not separate from it.

Think about the estrangement we experience from God, from each other and from the earth itself.

Pray for God's peace, justice and mercy to fill the earth.

As I look upon the oppression and exploitation that denies human dignity and violates the integrity of creation, I offer to You O God my hunger for justice.

Loving God, may justice flow like a mighty river through every aspect of human society; May your promise that the last shall be first be made real in the world today; May humanity's inhumanity be challenged and transformed in word and deed; And may the earth itself know freedom from the consequences of human greed and carelessness. Lord, in your mercy hear my prayer.

3rd January 2025
Hard Times

Joshua 1:9 "Have I not commanded you? Be strong and courageous! Do not tremble or be dismayed, for the Lord your God is with you wherever you go."

Crisis brings change

Sometimes God doesn't change your situation because he's trying to change your heart.

Pray

Loving God, I know that you are with me in every season of my life
Loving God, I know you love me completely.
Loving God, I know you will never leave me or abandon me to face difficult times alone.
Loving God, I know you will walk with me through the darkness.
Loving God, I know you will rejoice with me during the good times.
Loving God, I know you will walk with me on the hard path to find my way to holiness.
You are with me. You are there helping me.

4th January 2025
Encouragement During Hard Times

Psalm 55:22
Cast your burden on the LORD, and he will sustain you; he will never permit the righteous to be moved

Psalm 46:1
God is our refuge and strength, a very present help in trouble

We all have times in our lives when a trapdoor opens up under our feet and we plummet into agony, pain and suffering. It can be a death, the shock of having a life-changing illness or maybe the breakdown of a relationship or financial disaster.

It could be a day like any other until the trapdoor springs open. We all have trapdoors in our lives. If we are fortunate we may hear the hollow sound of the springs priming to open and jump off just in time: we defuse the argument with a smile or joke; we swerve to prevent the road accident that would have left our car crumpled up like a giant tin can. Sadly there will be a time when we thought we were standing on firm ground but the lever of the trapdoor jerks back. We remain frozen in mid-air for a fraction of a second, then we drop.

Pray

Loving God, Help me not to fear the future but to boldly trust that you are in control of my life. Calm me when my emotions plunge me down, and when I am in despair. There are times when I can't prayer, so please listen to my silent pain. Please help me to "Be still, and know that you are God". Be my comforter, my healer and bring me peace. In Jesus' name, Amen.

5th January 2025
Jeremiah 33:6 - God brings healing
Nevertheless, I will bring health and healing to it; I will heal my people and will let them enjoy abundant peace and security.

Mark 10:27
Jesus looked at them and said, 'With man this is impossible, but not with God; all things are possible with God'.

Perhaps your trapdoor experience was the diagnosis of a serious illness. Upon hearing the news there was a creak of wood, the sharp click of a sliding bolt, and then nothing but the sensation of rushing air. You fear a body that will be like a dying coral reef.

Although we are aware that complete physical healing may not always occur, we also know that God has a plan and a purpose for our lives.

A Prayer for Hard Times
Lord God, You know how difficult life is for me now. Please help me through this trial and tribulation. I know that at the end of this I will grow in faith but please be with me now. Please give me hope and mental relief to be able to sleep, eat and pray.

6th January 2025
In Genesis when the windows of the heavens open, the pouring rains are released. In Isaiah 24, the open windows of Heaven bring trembling to the Earth, in Malachi 3 we read if the windows of Heaven aren't opened, blessings won't be received. In 2 Kings 7, the windows of Heaven open to end a famine. *A translation calls these windows of Heaven - "Trapdoors opening in the sky.*

Looking back on your trapdoor experience, are there any positives you can find?

Pray

Loving God, you know my situation. You know me so well. Even the number of hairs on my head.

As the Good Shepherd, lead me to green pastures and still waters, restoring my soul and nurturing my spirit. Let me find solace and strength.

May the light of Your love shine upon me, illuminating my path and lifting me from the darkness of despair. Grant me hope and resilience as I journey through life's challenges.

Please God, show me how to be a good and faithful servant this year.

7th January 2025

We are in the midst of winter. Short days, long nights. Heavy, grey clouds and harsh winds sting our faces. Winter can be a time when you walk over frozen ground and you're sure nothing will ever grow again. Remember everyone has the wintertime of the soul.

What is God saying to you in the wintertime of your soul?

Pray
Loving God what are you saying to me in the wintertime of my faith?

8th January 2025

Luke 9:58
And Jesus said to him, "Foxes have holes, and birds of the air have nests, but the Son of Man has nowhere to lay his head."

Action

Be Socially Kind
Acknowledge rough sleepers by saying hello, asking them how they are, and stopping for a chat – it makes the world of difference. Having conversations helps to combat loneliness. Don't just ignore people.

A past volunteer for the charity Crisis over Christmas said: "One of the things our guests said they had enjoyed most about staying at the shelter over Christmas was the human contact - actually having conversations with people".

In a letter to the volunteers, one of the guests said they hadn't spoken to people like that in months. A few kind words and some genuine interest can make a real difference.

Pray

Gracious God, guide me to know how to help the homeless in our community. Lord, let the homeless find safety and comfort. Please God, help me not to be judgmental when I see a homeless person. Please show me ways to share Your love and glory. Almighty Father, bring warmth, safety, and nourishment to the homeless on the cold winter nights.

Consider the effects of light. It can warm and it can guide, but it can also expose and surprise. What does light in the darkness mean for the world? What does it mean for you?

9th January 2025

Psalm 28:6-7
Praise be to the LORD for He has heard my cry for mercy. The LORD is my strength and my shield; my heart trusts in him, and he helps me. My heart leaps for joy, and with my song I praise him.

While this entire verse is excellent, "The Lord is my strength and my shield…" is a particularly powerful section. When times are tough, the Lord will help give us the strength needed to carry on. It's important to never forget that.

A Prayer for Strength in Hard Times
Lord Jesus, fear has overcome me, it paralyses me. This is a hard time in my life. Please stand beside me and fill me with your strength and peace. Although I know Your voice, I lack the strength to do what needs to be done. I do not want to succumb to fear. Loving Father remove all fear and doubt. Uphold me and restore me to full strength, so that You can use me to advance the cause of Your kingdom, through Christ, our Savior. Amen.

10th January 2025

Psalm 82:3
Give justice to the weak and the fatherless; maintain the right of the afflicted and the destitute.

Proverbs 14:31
Whoever oppresses a poor man insults his Maker, but he who is generous to the needy honours him.

Action
A Smile and a Hot Drink
Many charities encourage passersby to offer people sleeping rough food or a drink, rather than money. But even if you don't do that, at least make some sort of acknowledgment. Nobody is fooled by you putting your head down or pretending to talk into your mobile phone. Even if you're not going to give something, look them in the

eye and say: 'No, sorry', because it's treating them on a human level.

Pray
Gracious God, bless the people who care for the homeless by making meals and providing shelter, clothing, and medical aid. Abba Father, please help me to know how to help the homeless people in my community. Please show me how to give them love and compassion without hurting their feelings and dignity.

11th January 2025

Psalm 62:5-8
Yes, my soul, find rest in God; my hope comes from him. Truly he is my rock and my salvation; he is my fortress, I shall not be shaken. My salvation and my honour depend on God; he is my mighty rock, my refuge. Trust in him at all times, you people; pour out your hearts to him, for God is our refuge.
Persistent, traumatic grief can cause us to go through the stages of grief: denial, anger, bargaining, depression and acceptance. These stages are our attempts to process change and protect ourselves while we adapt to a new reality.

Pray
Please, Loving Father, give me the courage to face up to the problems I have. I know that this time ahead will not be easy, but with the faith to know that you are there will give me the courage I need.

12th January 2025

Luke 3:10-11
And the crowds asked him, "What then shall we do?" And he answered them, "Whoever has two tunics is to share with him who has none, and whoever has food is to do likewise."

Matthew 8:20
And Jesus said to him, "Foxes have holes, and birds of the air have nests, but the Son of Man has nowhere to lay his head."

Proverbs 22:9

Whoever has a bountiful eye will be blessed, for he shares his bread with the poor.

Action
Donate Supplies
During the colder months, supplies can be a matter of life and death when living on the streets. While doing your Christmas shopping it's easy to order an extra item or two.

Hand warmers, baby wipes, sanitiser, bin bags, water bottles, socks and toiletries are of use to rough sleepers, as are larger items like a tent or sleeping bag. Ask them what they need and drop it off later. Clothes are of course handy, but make sure they're the right size.

Pray
Compassionate Father, I ask that You provide shelter for all the people who are homeless. It's unbearable to think of all the terrible conditions that they live in, the physical cold, the sorrow they must hold in their hearts. Guide them to safe shelters so they can be protected from the weather, from people with bad intentions, and from all other complications of living outdoors. Lord, please bless them and meet their needs. Please show me what I should do.

13th January 2025

Hebrews 13:5
God has said, 'Never will I leave you; never will I forsake you'.

God is always with us. Always remember that.

Being told of bad news can be like being given a passport to another country. It is unknown. 'Everyone who is born holds dual citizenship, in the kingdom of the well and the kingdom of the sick', writes Susan Sontag in her book Illness as Metaphor. 'Although we all prefer to use only the good passport, sooner or later each of us is obliged, at least for a spell, to identify ourselves as citizens of that other place.'

Pray

Thank you Gracious God for always being there for me. I'm finding it hard to process this difficult time in my life. Please give me the words to pray to you. Please provide someone for me to talk to about this.

14ᵗʰ January 2025
This Too Will Pass
1 Peter 5:10
"In His kindness God called you to share in His eternal glory by means of Christ Jesus. So after you have suffered a little while, He will restore, support, and strengthen you, and He will place you on a firm foundation."

2 Corinthians 1:10
"And He did rescue us from mortal danger, and He will rescue us again. We have placed our confidence in Him, and He will continue to rescue us."

Problems, trials, and suffering are all a part of life. As Christians, we can live with the promise that God, in His kindness, will use these things to strengthen us and produce fruit.

Pray
God of love, I thank you for another opportunity to be in Your presence. I thank You for Your grace and for Your mercy, Your protection and Your provision, for continuing to be faithful even when I am faithless. Above all I thank You for allowing me the privilege to know You. John says "no one can receive anything unless it is given from above." I love You because You first loved me and I can belong to this family of believers because You first called me.

15ᵗʰ January 2025

Jeremiah 29:11-13
"For I know the plans I have for you,' declares the LORD, 'plans to prosper you and not to harm you, plans to give you hope and a

future. Then you will call on me and come and pray to me, and I will listen to you. You will seek me and find me when you seek me with all your heart."

God has a plan for all of us and this verse from Jeremiah explains that perfectly.

When we trust in this plan and seek God with all our heart, good things will happen.

Life is full of ups and downs, and God is there for us in every single good and bad moment.

Pray

Thank you God for being there with me during the ups and downs of my life.

I know you have a plan and purpose for me.

Help me to seek you with all my heart.

Tell God about your ups and downs.

Trials & Tribulations

Counting my Blessings

16th January 2025

Matthew 6:19-20
"Do not lay up for yourselves treasures on earth, where moth and rust destroy and where thieves break in and steal, but lay up for yourselves treasures in heaven, where neither moth nor rust destroys and where thieves do not break in and steal.

Deuteronomy 15:11
For there will never cease to be poor in the land. Therefore I command you, 'You shall open wide your hand to your brother, to the needy and to the poor, in your land.'

Matthew 25:40
And the King will answer them, 'Truly, I say to you, as you did it to one of the least of these my brothers, you did it to me.'

Action
Volunteer
Larger charities like Crisis, Shelter and St Mungo's need an influx of nationwide volunteers for their winter programmes and help doing everything from serving food at soup kitchens to cleaning accommodation to providing activities and skill sessions. They need volunteers like hairdressers and assistants to chiropodists and dentists. There are cooking, laundry, cleaning and talking with the guests volunteering opportunities.

Pray
Loving God, strengthen the spirits every day and build the faith of people who have no homes. May they see the wonders of trusting You for all they need. Please provide people to help them.

Father of Compassion, I ask that You draw alongside these people and provide them with hope. Let them see brightness in their futures and encourage them. Show them ways to progress towards a better place, show them where to find food and clothes, and let them have faith to know that You will sustain them.

Please show me how I can encourage them.

What ARE ..... You Thankful for?

17ᵗʰ January 2025

Ezra 10:4 "Rise up…take courage and do it."

A great verse for those that need motivation, sometimes it takes a little grit and courage to get through things. God will help you find the courage you need to take on the challenges that lie ahead.

The problems of life can easily bear down on us sometimes and our peace can so quickly disappear. We can find it hard to find rest, physically, mentally and spiritually, when circumstances seem out of our control or when we face difficult decisions. When our mind is being attacked it brings added pressures such as fear and anxiety and we long for comfort and respite.

While thoughts are often focused on peace on earth, it's hard to strive for outward peace until peace is found within and with God.

Pray

Please God help me. I find it hard to find rest, physically, mentally and spiritually. Circumstances seem out of our control and I am facing difficult decisions. My mind is being attacked, I am under pressure and have fear and anxiety. Please provide me with comfort and respite.

18ᵗʰ January 2025

Galatians 6:2
Bear one another's burdens, and so fulfil the law of Christ.

Isaiah 58:10
If you pour yourself out for the hungry and satisfy the desire of the afflicted, then shall your light rise in the darkness and your gloom be as the noonday.

Prayer is a powerful way to show the love of Christ. We can pray silently, or in a whisper, or out loud. We can pray alone or in a group setting. If we can't find the words, the Holy Spirit will intercede on our behalf.

Pray for People Who Are Sick

Jesus, the Great Physician, please bless those who are ill or stricken with disease. In particular, I pray for the homeless who are sick. Whether it be a small sickness or a life-altering disease, I ask that You hear my prayer and bless them. Give them a strong will to keep going and build up their immune systems. Please provide help and encourage them to visit free clinics and guide them to free medical help. Please show me what I can do to help.

19th January 2025

How do you do a meditative walk?
Walk with intention.
Let yourself notice what is around you.
Tell God what you see.
Focus your attention.
Tell God what you are thinking
Feel your surroundings.
Notice when thoughts take over.
Bring your thoughts back to God.
Let yourself experience your surroundings.
Pause now and then and wait for what God is saying to you.

Pray

As I walk around your creation help me to notice you in it.

20th January 2025

Be Still

Psalm 46

1 God is our refuge and strength,
   an ever-present help in trouble.
2 Therefore we will not fear, though the earth give way
   and the mountains fall into the heart of the sea,
3 though its waters roar and foam

and the mountains quake with their surging.
4 There is a river whose streams make glad the city of God,
   the holy place where the Most High dwells.
5 God is within her, she will not fall;
   God will help her at break of day.
6 Nations are in uproar, kingdoms fall;
   he lifts his voice, the earth melts.

While Psalm 46 words span the centuries and generations it's easy to lose sight of the fact that God today is stable, unshakable and all powerful even in times of trouble (v2), when nature rages (v3), when war and conflict seem never ending (v6).

Pray

My God, glory and honour be unto You. Your word encourages me to enter into Your gates with thanksgiving in my heart and to enter Your presence with praise, for indeed today is another day that You have given to me, therefore should I not be glad and rejoice? I ask You to draw me ever closer to You, day by day, praying that I may become purer and live a better life.

21st January 2025

Today we focus our hearts on the "Lord of peace" who came down from heaven in the form of a baby. God knows that we are in a constant battle against fear! Fear wants to cripple us, to push us to react rather than carefully respond, and fear steals our joy. God has given us the gift of peace so we can live joy-filled lives!

For some people at this time, being still may mean an act of physically stopping, whether standing, or kneeling, or sitting. For others it may mean switching off electronic devices, taking time to breathe, taking a walk – whatever allows for this act of knowing that God is God. Recognising these moments is a habit that can be nurtured.

Pray

Please God let me be filled with a peace that surpasses my circumstances. I give thanks to the Lord for cancelling out fear and hopelessness with the sacrifice of his Son and promise of eternal life. Gracious God you know my fears that cripple me and steal my joy. Grant me the gift of peace so I can live a joy-filled life! Let me rejoice because I have an eternal hope in Jesus!

22nd January 2025

Isaiah 26:3
You will keep in perfect peace those whose minds are steadfast, because they trust in you.

Bookshops have never been so full of books on spirituality and religion. There's more and more content on mindfulness, the power of self, the supernatural, Buddhism, prayer ... and at the heart of it is that which humankind is constantly seeking – some form of inner peace.

Isaiah 26:3 reminds us that God 'will keep in perfect peace those whose minds are steadfast' or 'stayed on him' when we trust him. He is the source of peace, a relationship with him brings peace, serving him brings peace, trusting him brings peace.

Pray

Ask God for peace.

Kind and Loving God, in those times when I am anxious and tired and my mind is racing, I pray that you would lavish your peace on me, through your Holy Spirit.

Give me the strength to seek you, to trust you, to focus my thoughts and attention on you. In Jesus' name. Amen.

Changes Going Forward

23rd January 2025

Psalm 29:11 says, "The LORD gives strength to his people; the LORD blesses his people with peace."

Hope

Each day is an opportunity for hope

And hope will often arise from those deemed hopeless

Learn to hope in God even when hope seems impossible and beyond

Learn to hope in God's grace even when the rules of the world cry out that your values have no currency

Learn to hope in God's love

Hope as tender and ephemeral as a new shoot

But which can make the desert bloom and song birds return

Richard Carter
The City is my Monastery – A contemporary rule of life.
'Our place of retreat, our monastery, is here and now, where we are today'

Pray
Lord, bring your strength, peace and hope to your people! Let your presence be felt by all who seek you in a powerful way. Turn the hearts of mankind towards you. I pray that the lost turn to you and find an unshakable peace and hope that nothing else in this world can offer. Amen.

24th January 2025
Pathways To Prayer

Many Christians use a special "examen" (a Latin word for "a means of examining") prayer at the end of the day. An examen prayer has six simple steps:

1. Find a place to be still
Wherever you are, sit comfortably and be still. Relax, but try to be attentive to yourself and to God.

2. Give thanks for the good things of today
Recall one moment you are grateful for from today. Remember how you felt. Notice these feelings and reflect that all good things come from God. Offer your thanks.

3. Let go of things bothering you
What's on your mind at the moment? What is making you feel awkward or anxious? Raise these things to God and ask for the freedom that comes with the presence of the Holy Spirit.

4. Review your day
Try to recall the other events of the day. Reflect on what has happened and how you feel about it. Trust the Holy Spirit to show you the things that are important to think through and the insights that are important to know.

5. Talk with God
Tell God anything that comes to mind – jot it down, speak it out or think it through. God already knows our needs. This is to help us identify what we need to be aware of, let go or recognise.

6. Finish your prayer
An examen prayer can take a few minutes or a good hour. However long you have been able to give, offer this time to God with a closing prayer.

25th January 2025

Psalm 37:23-24
The LORD makes firm the steps of the one who delights in him; though he may stumble, he will not fall, for the LORD upholds him with his hand.
There may be many days when you have no time for a 'quiet time'. Such is the hustle and bustle of daily life that a day can fly by. Do remember, just one intentional pause for breath within the course of a hectic morning can return you to your Creator, if you're willing to take it. This can be an opportunity to create a small oasis of stillness within your day.

Pause, for a few moments.

Relax your shoulders.

Breathe, slowly and deeply.

Smile.

At times like this, our restless minds can find rest; and a space opens up, in which we become aware of the Presence that was here all along, waiting for us.

26th January 2025

Scripture shares how Jesus accepted help from others while He was travelling and sharing the message of God. When we help others, we are showing the love of God. The Bible tells us not to have a hard heart, but to be willing to help the poor (Deuteronomy 15:7-9).

Deuteronomy 15:7-9

7 If anyone is poor among your fellow Israelites in any of the towns of the land the LORD your God is giving you, do not be hard-hearted or tightfisted toward them.
8 Rather, be openhanded and freely lend them whatever they need.

Pray

In gratitude, I celebrate the hope and solace You provide, reminding me that You are my refuge and strength. I praise You and thank You for all Your goodness to me. I count out my blessing before You. I trust in Your love and rejoice in Your mercy.

'If I really wanted to pray I'll tell you what I'd do. I'd go out into a great big field all alone or into the deep, deep woods and I'd look up into that lovely blue sky that looks as if there was no end to its blueness and then I'd just feel a prayer.' That's a quote from Anne of Green Gables talking to Marilla.

Nature both help to keep us grounded, to remind us that there is so much more to life than the daily drudgery. At this time of year, it's particularly calming seeing the burnished reds and orange leaves on trees walking through the park, seeing dew drops on spiderwebs or the light dappling on the river and the sound of the birds. In moments like this we always feel closest to God and we are reminded how much natural beauty there is around us that we have a duty to protect and look after.

As the year turns, and the colours of autumn fade, here in the northern hemisphere the shorter and colder days and longer nights provide the backdrop for a deeper longing that the world's darkness and difficulty might be transformed by the dawning light of God's justice and mercy. One of the many traditional names for Jesus is the 'Dayspring' – the one who will bring in the everlasting day. Meanwhile in the darkness of early mornings, we, too, long for the warmth and light of God to embrace a cold, dark earth, not just in eternity, but here and now.

Who needs my help?

27th January 2025

Matthew 11:28
"Come to me, all you who are weary and burdened, and I will give you rest."

Pray
Almighty and everlasting God, you are always more ready to hear than I am to pray and to give more than either I desire or deserve: pour down upon us the abundance of your mercy, forgiving me those things of which my conscience is afraid and giving me those good things which I am not worthy to ask but through the merits and mediation of Jesus Christ your Son our Lord, who is alive and reigns with you, Amen.

28th January 2025

Isaiah 40:28-31
"Do you not know? Have you not heard? The LORD is the everlasting God, the Creator of the ends of the earth. He will not grow tired or weary, and his understanding no one can fathom. He gives strength to the weary and increases the power of the weak. Even youths grow tired and weary, and young men stumble and fall; but those who hope in the LORD will renew their strength. They will soar on wings like eagles; they will run and not grow weary, they will walk and not be faint."

While this reading is inspiring, the "soar on wings like eagles" is particularly encouraging. If you need the strength to get through something tough, then place your hope in the Lord.

Pray

Dear God, I thank you for all your goodness and kindness to me. I pray that my spirit may soar like eagles. I place my faith and hope in you, Loving God, to give me strength and courage for the times ahead.

Rejoice

IN THE *Lord* ALWAYS.
I WILL SAY IT AGAIN:

Rejoice!

-PHILIPPIANS 4:4

Ways for Me to Pray

29th January 2025

Pathway to Prayers
Intercessory Prayers
Intercessory prayer is the act of praying to God on behalf of others. In the Old Testament, the prophets – Ezekiel, Joel, Deborah, Habakkuk, Samuel and Hosea all interceded for nations. They called for, among other things, forgiveness, judgement, mercy, and an end to drought.

In the New Testament, Paul repeatedly asks for prayers and also teaches that we should 'carry each other's burdens, and in this way you will fulfil the law of Christ.' (Galatians 6:2).

There are so many challenging situations across the world. Ask God to place a country or situation on your heart. Spend some time listening and reflecting on what he shares with you. Begin by acknowledging God's power. Then pray general prayers: pray for God's kingdom to come; pray for individuals and communities; pray for those in power.

Pray that local churches will be a beacon of hope in their communities. Ask that they will be filled with God's love and that the Holy Spirit will guide and strengthen them as they support people in practical and spiritual ways. Keep inviting the Holy Spirit to speak into the situations you are praying for.

Listen to what God is saying. Make time each week to pray about this country or situation. You could set a reminder on your phone or put a sticky note in your Bible to remind you. Use your prayer journal to write down your petitions and answers to prayers. Stick a map of the country to your fridge and attach sticky notes of your prayer.

Examples of Intercessory Prayers

Lord, save our rulers! Answer us in the day we call! (Psalm 20:9)

Save your people, and bless the people that belong to you. Shepherd them, and carry them forever. (Psalm 28:9)

Give us peace in our time, For there is no one who fights for us but you, O Lord. (from 2 Chronicles 20:15)

30th January 2025

Do not be anxious about anything (Philippians 4:6-7)
Do not be anxious about anything, but in every situation, by prayer and petition, with thanksgiving, present your requests to God. And the peace of God, which transcends all understanding, will guard your hearts and your minds in Christ Jesus.

Quite often we have little control over the lack of external peace in our immediate surroundings and globally, but we can have control over our own inner peace.

Most of us can't simply stop being anxious. What we can do is to focus this energy on taking our concerns to God in the form of prayer and practicing being thankful. By doing this we can experience Christ's peace, which will guard our emotions and our minds.

Take some moments to honestly assess the condition of your mind right now.
Is it full of the 'stuff of life'?
What do the words 'Do not be anxious' mean to you in your current state of mind?

It is one of the most common commands in the bible.

What would it look like for you to claim this promise for your own life right now?

Pray about this.

Please Help Me

31st January 2025

During this time, following these readings, has it helped you become more aware of God's presence in your life, and in the people and events of your life? Each person's experience is different, so each of us needs to find the best way for nurturing and continuing our walk with God.

Looking Back Over the Last 2 Months
What have you learnt about your relationship with God?
What will you take forward with you in your relationship with God?

Looking Back

How is God Changing Me?

How Can I Serve God?

Changes Going Forward

Thoughts & Prayers

Answers to Prayers

Preparing for Lent

If daily readings aid your Christian journey then the next event in the Christian calendar is Lent. Lent is a time of 40 days when we open ourselves up to God for his examination. Lent is a season that prepares our hearts for the celebration of Easter, much like Advent prepares us for Christmas.

In 2025, Lent is from Ash Wednesday on 5th March 2025 to Easter Sunday 20th April 2025

There are free eBooks to download for 5 days from Sunday 2nd March 2025 at Lent Publications on Amazon. Please follow Lent Publications on Amazon. Please leave a positive review.

For
God
so loved the world,
that He gave His only begotten Son,
that
whosoever
believeth in
Him should
not perish,
but have
everlasting
life.
JOHN 3:16

Printed in Great Britain
by Amazon

48433979R00066